Bill Walsh

REMEMBERING
"THE GENIUS"
1931-2007

ISBN 13: 978-1-59670-323-0

Front cover and title page photo by Mike Powell/Getty Images
Back cover photo by Michael Zagaris/Getty Images

SportsPublishingLLC.com

Publishers: Peter L. Bannon and Joseph J. Bannon Sr.
Senior managing editor: Susan M. Moyer
Contributing writer and editor: Steve Contorno
Art director and cover design: Dustin J. Hubbart
Photo editor: Jessica Martinich
Graphic design: Joseph T. Brumleve

Sports Publishing L.L.C.
804 North Neil Street
Champaign, IL 61820
Phone: 1-877-424-2665
Fax: 217-363-2073
SportsPublishingLLC.com

Printed in the United States of America

3

"Bill pushed us all to be perfect because that's all he ever knew. This is a tremendous loss for all of us, especially to the Bay Area, because of what he meant to the 49ers. Outside of my father, he was the most influential person in my life. I'm going to miss him."
—Joe Montana

"The one thing that sticks in my mind about playing for Bill was how unfair it was, because we had such an advantage over the people we were playing. Not everyone wanted to admit that."
—Randy Cross

"Bill basically taught us how to be professional on and off the field. He was a visionary. A motivator. An innovator. He was ahead of his time."
—Roger Craig

"What really made Bill special is that he understood that the game was bigger than him. His genius was not centered around Xs and Os; it was centered around his ability to create a platform that made the game inclusive to others."
—Ronnie Lott

"He was the most important person in football over the last 25 years, and I don't think there's any debate about that. He brought into Silicon Valley, about the time Silicon Valley was being born, the same kind of innovation. . . . I've always said Bill would have been a great CEO of anything. Luckily for us, it was the 49ers."
—Steve Young

"He was an innovative, optimistic, high-principled and highly motivated master of the game. He played by the rules, and he cared deeply about the players, the coaches, the fans and about the game itself."
—Marv Levy

"I always said that he was an artist and all the rest of us were blacksmiths pounding the anvil, while he was painting the picture."
—Mike Holmgren

"He was one of the most creative people in the sport. Everywhere he went he was a winner. He was one of those unusual people who could say, 'Here's a play, it's going to work, and here's what's going to happen.' That's one of the hardest things in football."
—Joe Gibbs

"He was an innovative guy who brought his philosophy to the NFL, and he integrated the right people into it and allowed it to flourish. He is one of the very few people who really helped make the NFL what it is today, and his coaching tree is evidence of that."
—Bill Parcells

"He was a great competitor and was one of the most innovative coaches in the game. The offensive philosophy that he installed in those great 49er teams more than 25 years ago will remain his legacy and is still very much a part of the NFL to this day."
—Don Shula

BILL WALSH:
A LIFE IN
FOOTBALL

1977-78	Head coach – Stanford
1979-88	Head coach – San Francisco 49ers
1992-94	Head coach – Stanford
1996	Special assistant to the offense – San Francisco 49ers
1999-01	General manager – San Francisco 49ers
2004-06	Special assistant to Athletic Director – Stanford
2006	Interim Athletic Director – Stanford
2006-07	Special assistant to Athletic Director – Stanford

THE
SAN FRANCISCO
YEARS

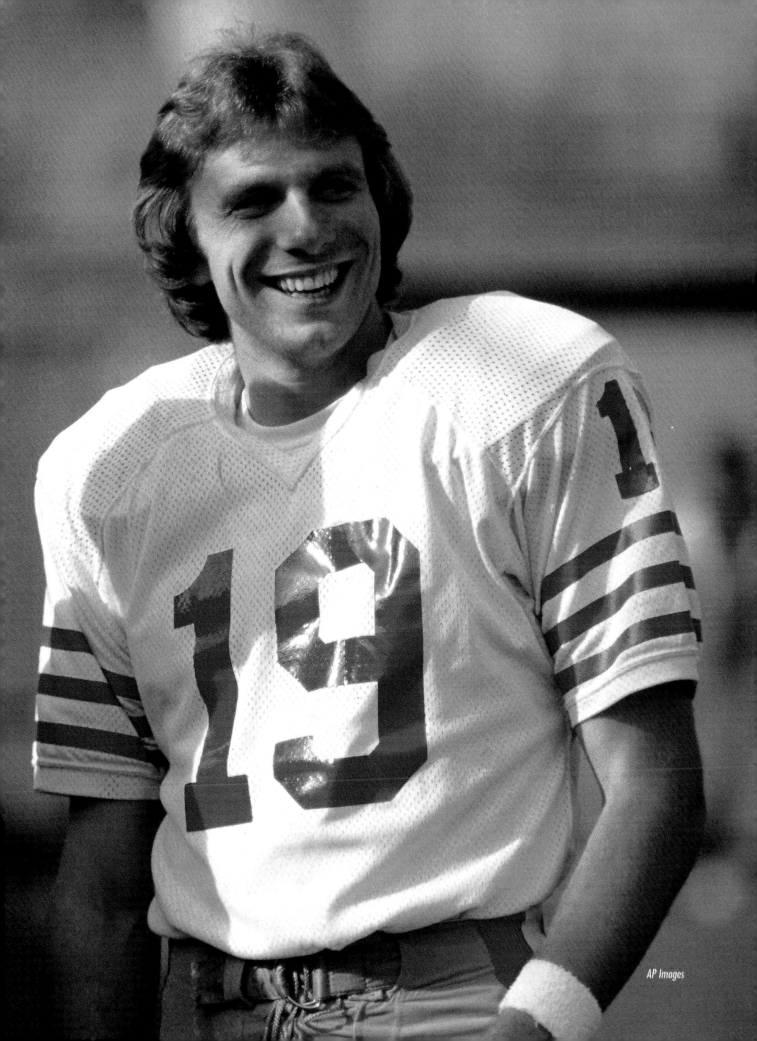

WALSH LEAVES INDELIBLE MARK

—— BY JANIE McCAULEY, AP SPORTS WRITER ——

Bill Walsh could be as serious as they come and he could be down right hilarious. He could be creative and he could be precise.

For those whose lives he touched, the Hall of Fame football coach will be remembered as a teacher who cared deeply about his players and many others whose path he crossed—a man who found new ways to win.

"Bill Walsh personified what it meant to be a human being," said Jim Harbaugh, Stanford's new football coach who knew Walsh for 18 years and once received footwork tips from the coach while playing for the Bears. "Everything that came out of his mind, his heart, his mouth, I hung on every single word."

Nicknamed "The Genius" for his original schemes that became known as the West Coast Offense, Walsh died at his Woodside home Monday morning following a long battle with leukemia. He was 75.

Walsh changed the NFL with his innovative offense and a legion of coaching disciples, breaking new ground and winning three Super Bowls with the San Francisco 49ers along the way.

Jerry Rice remembers the time Walsh stood in as a bellman at a hotel and started carrying bags, and the day he showed up at practice sporting tights to match those worn by Rice.

"It blew me away," Rice recalled with a grin. "You have to have a certain body to wear tights."

But most of all, Rice cherishes the chance Walsh gave him. The San Francisco

49ers selected the wide receiver out of Mississippi Valley State in the first round back in 1985.

"He gave me the opportunity to come to a winner, San Francisco out of Mississippi Valley State University," Rice said. "I was the 16th player taken in the first round. It was all because of Bill Walsh and what he stood for. I think that was very unique for him, because he could see talent."

Walsh didn't become an NFL head coach until 47, and he spent just 10 seasons on the San Francisco sideline. But he left an indelible mark on the nation's most popular sport, building the once-woebegone 49ers into the most successful team of the 1980s.

"THE ESSENCE OF BILL WALSH WAS THAT HE WAS AN EXTRAORDINARY TEACHER."
— NFL COMMISSIONER ROGER GOODELL

The soft-spoken Californian also produced an army of proteges. Many of his former assistants went on to lead their own teams, handing down Walsh's methods to dozens more coaches in a tree with innumerable branches.

"The essence of Bill Walsh was that he was an extraordinary teacher," NFL commissioner Roger Goodell said.

Walsh went 102-63-1 with the 49ers, winning 10 of his 14 postseason games along with six division titles. He was the NFL's coach of the year in 1981 and 1984.

Few men did more to shape the look of football into the 21st century. His cerebral nature and often-brilliant stratagems earned him his nickname well before his election to the Pro Football Hall of Fame in 1993.

"This is just a tremendous loss for all of us, especially to the Bay Area because of what he meant to the 49ers," said Joe Montana, San Francisco's Hall of Fame quarterback. "Outside of my dad he was probably the most influential person in my life. I am going to miss him."

Walsh visited with friends until the end, and attended basketball games at Stanford all winter. Tyrone Willingham, now the coach at Washington, and Stanford donor and alumnus John Arrillaga went to see Walsh on Sunday, pre-

Michael Zagaris/Getty Images

Bill Walsh, quarterback Joe Montana, and 49ers owner Ed Debartolo Jr. pose with the Lombardi Trophy after winning Super Bowl XIX. *AP Images*

senting him with the Stagg Award for his outstanding service to football.

Walsh created the Minority Coaching Fellowship program in 1987, helping minority coaches get a foothold in a previously white-dominated profession. Willingham and Marvin Lewis were among those who went through the program, later adopted as a league-wide initiative.

"The world lost a great man in Bill Walsh. He had a tremendous impact on me, both personally and professionally," said Willingham, who replaced Walsh as Stanford's head coach in 1994. "Bill's development of the minority coaching program at the collegiate and professional levels literally changed the face of football."

Raiders owner Al Davis and Hall of Famer John Madden stopped by to see Walsh on Saturday, and Montana on Friday and also last Wednesday along with

"THE WORLD LOST A GREAT MAN IN BILL WALSH. HE HAD A TREMENDOUS IMPACT ON ME, BOTH PERSONALLY AND PROFESSIONALLY."
— TYRONE WILLINGHAM

Ronnie Lott. Hall of Fame quarterback Steve Young was planning to see Walsh on Monday when he received the sad news instead.

"He knew me well before I knew myself and knew what I could accomplish well before I knew that I could accomplish it," Young said. "That's a coach. That's the ultimate talent anyone could have. I said in my Hall of Fame speech that he was the most important person in football in the last 25 years, and I don't think there's any debate about that."

Walsh twice served as the 49ers' general manager, and coach George Seifert led San Francisco to two more Super Bowl titles after Walsh left the sideline. Walsh also coached Stanford during two terms over five seasons.

Even a short list of Walsh's adherents is stunning. Seifert, Mike Holmgren, Dennis Green, Sam Wyche, Ray Rhodes and Bruce Coslet all became NFL head coaches after serving on Walsh's San Francisco staffs, and Tony Dungy played for him. Most of his former assistants passed on Walsh's structures and strategies to a new generation of coaches, including Mike Shanahan, Jon Gruden, Brian

Billick, Andy Reid, Pete Carroll, Gary Kubiak, Steve Mariucci and Jeff Fisher.

In 2004, Walsh was diagnosed with leukemia—the disease that also killed his son, former ABC News reporter Steve Walsh, in 2002 at age 46. Walsh underwent months of treatment and blood transfusions, and publicly disclosed his illness in November 2006.

Born William Ernest Walsh on November 30, 1931, in Los Angeles, Walsh's family moved to the Bay Area when he was a teenager.

He was a self-described "average" end at San Jose State in 1952-53. He married his college sweetheart, Geri Nardini, in 1954 and started his coaching career at Washington High School in Fremont, leading the football and swim teams.

Walsh was coaching in Fremont when Marv Levy, then the coach at the University of California, hired him as an assistant.

Walsh did a stint at Stanford before beginning his pro coaching career as an assistant with the AFL's Oakland Raiders in 1966, forging a friendship with Davis that endured through decades of rivalry. Walsh joined the Cincinnati Bengals in 1968 to work for legendary coach Paul Brown, who gradually gave complete control of the Bengals' offense to his assistant.

Walsh built a playbook that included short dropbacks and novel receiving routes, as well as

Bill Walsh gives a pregame speech as John Ayers (68), assistant coach Paul Hackett, Randy Cross (51), Dwight Clark, Freddie Solomon, and Mike Wilson (85) listen.

Michael Zagaris/Getty Images

> "WHEN WRITING HIS SCRIPT, HE DIDN'T BELIEVE THAT RUNNING THE FOOTBALL WAS THE WAY TO GET THERE. IT HAD TO BE PRETTIER THAN THAT—BEAUTIFUL IN SOME WAY."
>
> — KEENA TURNER

constant repetition of every play in practice. Though it originated in Cincinnati, it became known many years later as the West Coast Offense—a name Walsh never liked or repeated, but which eventually grew to encompass his offensive philosophy and the many tweaks added by Holmgren, Shanahan and others.

"He was a perfectionist," said Keena Turner, a linebacker with the Niners for 11 years before going on to coach. "When writing his script, he didn't believe that running the football was the way to get there. It had to be prettier than that—beautiful in some way."

By the 1990s, much of the NFL was running some version of the West Coast Offense, with its fundamental belief that the passing game can set up an effective running attack, rather than the opposite conventional wisdom.

Walsh also is widely credited with inventing or

Bill Walsh addresses his team from atop a stool before playing the Pittsburgh Steelers. *Michael Zagaris/Getty Images*

Bill Walsh, Chuck Noll, Larry Little, and Dan Fouts are introduced as the Pro Football Hall of Fame Class of 1993 on the field before the NFL Pro Bowl. *NFL Images/Getty Images*

popularizing many of the modern basics of coaching, from the laminated sheets of plays held by coaches on almost every sideline, to the practice of scripting the first 15 offensive plays of a game.

After a bitter falling-out with Brown in 1976, Walsh left for stints with the San Diego Chargers and Stanford before the 49ers chose him to rebuild the franchise in 1979.

The long-suffering team had gone 2-14 before Walsh's arrival. The Niners repeated the record in his first season. Walsh doubted his abilities to turn around such a miserable situation—but earlier in 1979, the 49ers drafted Montana from Notre Dame.

Walsh turned over the starting job to Montana in 1980, when the 49ers improved to 6-10—and improbably, San Francisco won its first championship in 1981, just two years after winning two games.

Championships followed in the postseasons of 1984 and 1988 as Walsh built a consistent winner. He also showed considerable acumen in personnel, adding Lott, Charles Haley, Roger Craig and Rice to his rosters after he was named the 49ers' general manager in 1982 and then president in 1985.

"I came to San Francisco, and I found another father, Bill Walsh," Rice said.

Walsh left the 49ers with a profound case of burnout after his third Super Bowl victory in January 1989, though he later regretted not coaching longer.

He spent three years as a broadcaster with NBC before returning to Stanford for three seasons. He then took charge of the 49ers' front office in 1999, helping to rebuild the roster over three seasons. But Walsh gradually cut ties with the 49ers after his hand-picked successor as GM, Terry Donahue, took over in 2001.

He is survived by his wife, Geri, and two children, Craig and Elizabeth. ✦

THE WEST COAST WAY

S everal coaches in football history have muttered the phrase, "There are three things that can happen when you throw a pass, and two of them are bad."

Bill Walsh was not one of them. Known as a great innovator and a genius in his own right, Walsh developed a new offense based on the very thing those coaches feared: the forward pass.

According to football lore, the first pass was thrown in a 1905 game between Saint Louis University and Carroll College. Neither school would soon set a trend, however, as the sport remained running oriented for well into the second half of the 20th century. Walsh's West Coast Offense shifted the game to an aerial sport, opening up the playbooks for systems today that predominantly feature passing plays.

The West Coast offense reversed old football thinking that declared a team needed to first establish the run in order to open up the pass. Walsh instead used short, horizontal passes to spread out the defense, relying on his receivers to gain yards after the catch. The system was based on short timing routes and three- to five-step drops to get rid of the ball quickly. Defenses would subsequently focus on those short routes, opening up the opportunities to run the ball or throw it deep.

But the West Coast offense was a philosophy as much as a scheme. It preached precision and preparation. Walsh was meticulous with his play calling, often scripting the first 15-25 plays of the game ahead of time. This allowed him to gauge the defense's tendencies as the game unfolded so he could exploit them later. That ability—to recognize the holes and weaknesses in a defense and react accordingly—is just as important as the plays themselves in a West Coast offense. Bill Walsh was superior in making such assessments, and for this reason his genius went beyond the Xs and Os.

His system also relied on running backs who could catch the ball out of the backfield. For the 49ers, Walsh enlisted Roger Craig to be that back. Craig's versatility—in 1985 he gained 1,000 yards both on the ground and receiving—was exactly what Walsh required to complete his West Coast offense. On any given play, a running back could be asked to fulfill the role of receiver, positioning speedy backs against slower linebackers to predictable results.

The West Coast system, while used to perfection by Walsh, Joe Montana, and the 49ers, has

Walsh talks on the sidelines with Joe Montana and Steve Young during the NFC Divisional Playoff against the Minnesota Vikings in 1989.
Arthur Anderson/NFL Images/Getty Images

been modified and recycled to this day. After Walsh retired, George Seifert took over as San Francisco's coach and used the system with Steve Young to win two Super Bowls. Mike Shannahan, Mike Holmgren, and Jon Gruden have all also used the system, with notable success.

Today, the term West Coast offense seems to be used loosely to describe any team that favors the pass over the run. But its roots lie with Walsh, the ultimate trendsetter, who transformed the game from a ground game into an aerial assault.

There are three things that can happen when you throw a forward pass. One of them is winning championships. ✦

Running back O.J. Simpson.
Michael Zagaris/Getty Images

1979

RECORD 2-14

NFC WEST	W	L	T	W%	PF	PA
Los Angeles Rams	9	7	0	.563	323	309
New Orleans Saints	8	8	0	.500	370	360
Atlanta Falcons	6	10	0	.375	300	388
San Francisco 49ers	**2**	**14**	**0**	**.125**	**308**	**416**

SCHEDULE

Week 1	SFO	22	at MIN	28
Week 2	DAL	21	at SFO	13
Week 3	SFO	24	at LAM	27
Week 4	NOR	30	at SFO	21
Week 5	SFO	9	at SDG	31
Week 6	SEA	35	at SFO	24
Week 7	SFO	16	at NYG	32
Week 8	ATL	15	at SFO	20
Week 9	CHI	28	at SFO	27
Week 10	SFO	10	at OAK	23
Week 11	SFO	20	at NOR	31
Week 12	DEN	38	at SFO	28
Week 13	LAM	26	at SFO	20
Week 14	SFO	10	at SLC	13
Week 15	TAM	7	at SFO	23
Week 16	SFO	21	at ATL	31

1979 DRAFT

RND	PICK#	PLAYER, COLLEGE
2	29	James Owens, UCLA
3	82	Joe Montana, Notre Dame
5	111	Tom Seabron, Michigan
5	119	Jerry Aldridge, Angelo State
6	138	Ruben Vaughan, Colorado
7	166	Phil Francis, Stanford
9	221	Steve Hamilton, Missouri
10	249	Dwight Clark, Clemson
10	252	Howard Ballage, Colorado
11	276	Billy McBride, Tenn. State

TEAM OFFENSE

	PASSING						RUSHING				TOTAL
	CMP	ATT	YD	YPA	TD	INT	ATT	YD	YPA	TD	YD
TOTALS	361	602	3,760	6.25	18	21	480	1,932	4.03	17	5,692
NFL RANK	1	1	6	22	15	10	26	20	13	11	8

TEAM DEFENSE

	PASSING						RUSHING				TOTAL
	CMP	ATT	YD	YPA	TD	INT	ATT	YD	YPA	TD	YD
TOTALS	262	441	3407	7.73	25	15	544	2213	4.07	24	5620
NFL RANK	20	9	23	26	26	24	18	15	17	25	20

Defensive tackle Archie Reese (78) holds the game ball in the locker room following the 49ers' 38-35 win over the Saints during the 1980 season. San Francisco trailed 35-7 before completing what many consider to be the greatest regular-season comeback in NFL history.
Michael Zagaris/Getty Images

1980

RECORD 6-10

NFC WEST	W	L	T	W%	PF	PA
Atlanta Falcons	12	4	0	.750	405	272
Los Angeles Rams	11	5	0	.688	424	289
San Francisco 49ers	**6**	**10**	**0**	**.375**	**320**	**415**
New Orleans Saints	1	15	0	.063	291	487

SCHEDULE

Week 1	SFO	26	at NOR	23
Week 2	SLC	21	at SFO	24
Week 3	SFO	37	at NYJ	27
Week 4	ATL	20	at SFO	17
Week 5	SFO	26	at LAM	48
Week 6	SFO	14	at DAL	59
Week 7	LAM	31	at SFO	17
Week 8	TAM	24	at SFO	23
Week 9	SFO	13	at DET	17
Week 10	SFO	16	at GNB	23
Week 11	SFO	13	at MIA	17
Week 12	NYG	0	at SFO	12
Week 13	NWE	17	at SFO	21
Week 14	NOR	35	at SFO	38
Week 15	SFO	10	at ATL	35
Week 16	BUF	18	at SFO	13

1980 DRAFT

RND	PICK#	PLAYER, COLLEGE
1	13	Earl Cooper, Rice
1	20	Jim Stuckey, Clemson
2	39	Keena Turner, Purdue
3	65	Jim Miller, Mississippi
3	77	Craig Puki, Tennessee
4	84	Ricky Churchman, Texas
4	98	David Hodge, Houston
5	112	Kenneth Times, Southern
6	139	Herb Williams, Southern
8	210	Bobby Leopold, Notre Dame
9	237	Dan Hartwig, Cal.-Lutheran

TEAM OFFENSE

	PASSING						RUSHING				TOTAL
	CMP	ATT	YD	YPA	TD	INT	ATT	YD	YPA	TD	YD
TOTALS	363	597	3,799	6.36	27	26	415	1,743	4.20	10	5,542
NFL RANK	1	1	6	25	8	24	27	24	7	24	12

TEAM DEFENSE

	PASSING						RUSHING				TOTAL
	CMP	ATT	YD	YPA	TD	INT	ATT	YD	YPA	TD	YD
TOTALS	327	495	3,958	8.00	29	17	556	2,218	3.99	20	6,176
NFL RANK	24	15	26	28	27	24	23	23	19	26	27

Wide receiver Dwight Clark makes "The Catch" against the Dallas Cowboys in the final seconds to clinch the NFC Championship on January 10, 1982.
B Bennett/Getty Images

1981

RECORD 13-3

NFC WEST	W	L	T	W%	PF	PA
San Francisco 49ers	**13**	**3**	**0**	**.813**	**357**	**250**
Atlanta Falcons	7	9	0	.438	426	355
Los Angeles Rams	6	10	0	.375	303	351
New Orleans Saints	4	12	0	.250	207	378

SCHEDULE

Week 1	SFO	17	at DET	24
Week 2	CHI	17	at SFO	28
Week 3	SFO	17	at ATL	34
Week 4	NOR	14	at SFO	21
Week 5	SFO	30	at WAS	17
Week 6	DAL	14	at SFO	45
Week 7	SFO	13	at GNB	3
Week 8	LAM	17	at SFO	20
Week 9	SFO	17	at PIT	14
Week 10	ATL	14	at SFO	17
Week 11	CLE	15	at SFO	12
Week 12	SFO	33	at LAM	31
Week 13	NYG	10	at SFO	17
Week 14	SFO	21	at CIN	3
Week 15	HOO	6	at SFO	28
Week 16	SFO	21	at NOR	17
NFC Div. Playoff	NYG	24	at SFO	38
NFC Championship	DAL	27	at SFO	28
Super Bowl XVI	CIN	21	at SFO	26

1981 DRAFT

RND	PICK#	PLAYER, COLLEGE
1	8	Ronnie Lott, USC
2	36	John Harty, Iowa
2	40	Eric Wright, Missouri
3	65	Carlton Williamson, Pittsburgh
5	121	Lynn Thomas, Pittsburgh
5	122	Arrington Jones, Winston-Salem State
6	147	Pete Kugler, Penn State
8	203	Garry White, Minnesota
11	286	Rob DeBose, UCLA
12	313	Major Ogilvie, Alabama
12	322	Joe Adams, Tennessee State

TEAM OFFENSE

	PASSING						RUSHING				TOTAL
	CMP	ATT	YD	YPA	TD	INT	ATT	YD	YPA	TD	YD
TOTALS	328	517	3,766	7.28	20	13	560	1,941	3.47	17	5,707
NFL RANK	5	9	8	9	17	2	6	19	28	11	14

TEAM DEFENSE

	PASSING						RUSHING				TOTAL
	CMP	ATT	YD	YPA	TD	INT	ATT	YD	YPA	TD	YD
TOTALS	273	514	3,135	6.10	16	27	464	1,918	4.13	10	5,053
NFL RANK	11	19	4	3	7	5	2	12	21	5	2

SUPER BOWL XVI

JANUARY 24, 1982
PONTIAC SILVERDOME · PONTIAC, MICHIGAN

	1	2	3	4	T
San Francisco 49ers	7	13	0	6	26
Cincinnati Bengals	0	0	7	14	21

Following one of the most acclaimed conference championships of all time—San Francisco's 28-27 win over Dallas—Super Bowl XVI flirted with the anticlimactic. The 49ers had made it to the big game on a play so outstanding it defied description, going down in football lore simply as "The Catch." The famous drive that lead to the 49ers' last-second win over the Cowboys set up a contest between young, pass-happy San Francisco and the veteran, well-balanced Cincinnati Bengals. Both teams were similar in that they posted 6-10 records the previous season, had strong offensive lines, and boasted better-than-average defenses. But in the end, few failed to distinguish the better team as the 49ers notched a 26-21 victory. San Francisco built its first-half lead on the meticulous play of game MVP Joe Montana, appearing in his first Super Bowl just three seasons into his career. The 49ers struck first when Montana scored on a one-yard run on the team's first drive, highlighted by a fake-reverse flea flicker. In the second quarter Montana connected on an 11-yard touchdown pass to fullback Earl Cooper to complete a 92-yard drive, then led his team on two more scoring drives that resulted in field goals. By halftime, the Bengals were already staring down a Super Bowl-record 20-point deficit. The Bengals would rally, however, making a game of it for the 40 million households that tuned in to make Super Bowl XVI the fourth-most-watched TV event in history up to that point. Cincinnati scored in the third quarter on a five-yard run by quarterback Ken Anderson, then again early in the fourth when Anderson connected on a pass to Dan Ross. The 49ers responded with two field goals by Ray Wersching to pad their lead to 26-14. The Bengals scored a meaningless touchdown in the final moments of the game to bring them to within five. But victory went to the 49ers, who became the first team in Super Bowl history to win the game despite being outgained from the line of scrimmage (356 yards to 275). San Francisco's defense forced one turnover after another to negate the Bengals' advantage in yardage and keep them out of the end zone. By the time Pat Summerall and John Madden signed off for CBS, the 49ers were well into their celebration of the team's first NFL championship.

OPPOSITE TOP: Bill Walsh is carried off the field after Super Bowl XVI. *Focus on Sport/Getty Images*

OPPOSITE BOTTOM: Keena Turner celebrates the 49ers win in Super Bowl XVI. *Andy Hayt/Getty Images*

1982

RECORD 3-6

NFC STANDINGS (shortened season due to strike)

TEAM	W	L	T	W%	PF	PA
Washington Redskins	8	1	0	.889	190	128
Dallas Cowboys	6	3	0	.667	226	145
Atlanta Falcons	5	4	0	.556	183	199
Green Bay Packers	5	3	1	.556	226	169
Minnesota Vikings	5	4	0	.556	187	198
St. Louis Cardinals	5	4	0	.556	135	170
Tampa Bay Buccaneers	5	4	0	.556	158	178
Detroit Lions	4	5	0	.444	181	176
New Orleans Saints	4	5	0	.444	129	160
New York Giants	4	5	0	.444	164	160
Chicago Bears	3	6	0	.333	141	174
Philadelphia Eagles	3	6	0	.333	191	195
San Francisco 49ers	**3**	**6**	**0**	**.333**	**209**	**206**
Los Angeles Rams	2	7	0	.222	200	250

SCHEDULE

Week 1	LAD	23	at SFO	17
Week 2	SFO	21	at DEN	24
Week 11	SFO	31	at SLC	20
Week 12	NOR	23	at SFO	20
Week 13	SFO	30	at LAM	24
Week 14	SDG	41	at SFO	37
Week 15	ATL	17	at SFO	7
Week 16	SFO	26	at KAN	13
Week 17	LAM	21	at SFO	20

1982 DRAFT

RND	PICK#	PLAYER, COLLEGE
2	29	Bubba Paris, Michigan
5	139	Newton Williams, Ariz. State
6	151	Vince Williams, Oregon
7	195	Ron Ferrari, Illinois
9	251	Bryan Clark, Michigan State
10	269	Dana McLemore, Hawaii
10	279	Tim Barbian, Western Illinois
11	306	Gary Gibson, Arizona
12	334	Tim Washington, Fresno State

TEAM OFFENSE

	PASSING						RUSHING				TOTAL
	CMP	ATT	YD	YPA	TD	INT	ATT	YD	YPA	TD	YD
TOTALS	215	348	2,668	7.67	17	11	219	740	3.38	6	3,408
NFL RANK	2	1	2	7	3	10	27	28	28	19	5

TEAM DEFENSE

	PASSING						RUSHING				TOTAL
	CMP	ATT	YD	YPA	TD	INT	ATT	YD	YPA	TD	YD
TOTALS	158	278	1,949	7.01	14	9	303	1,199	3.96	9	3,148
NFL RANK	16	12	13	14	23	25	23	21	20	18	20

John Kelly/Getty Images

1983

RECORD 10-6

NFC WEST	W	L	T	W%	PF	PA
San Francisco 49ers	**10**	**6**	**0**	**.625**	**432**	**293**
Los Angeles Rams	9	7	0	.563	361	344
New Orleans Saints	8	8	0	.500	319	337
Atlanta Falcons	7	9	0	.438	370	389

SCHEDULE

Week 1	PHI	22	at SFO	17
Week 2	SFO	48	at MIN	17
Week 3	SFO	42	at SLC	27
Week 4	ATL	20	at SFO	24
Week 5	SFO	33	at NWE	13
Week 6	LAM	10	at SFO	7
Week 7	SFO	32	at NOR	13
Week 8	SFO	45	at LAM	35
Week 9	NYJ	27	at SFO	13
Week 10	MIA	20	at SFO	17
Week 11	NOR	0	at SFO	27
Week 12	SFO	24	at ATL	28
Week 13	SFO	3	at CHI	31
Week 14	TAM	21	at SFO	35
Week 15	SFO	23	at BUF	10
Week 16	DAL	17	at SFO	42
NFC Div. Playoff	DET	23	at SFO	24
NFC Championship	SFO	21	at WAS	24

1983 DRAFT

RND	PICK#	PLAYER, COLLEGE
2	49	Roger Craig, Nebraska
3	59	Blanchard Montgomery, UCLA
4	90	Tom Holmoe, Brigham Young
5	117	Riki Ellison, USC
7	175	Gary Moten, Southern Methodist
9	229	Mike Mularkey, Florida
10	259	Jeff Merrill, Nebraska
11	289	Jesse Sapolu, Hawaii

TEAM OFFENSE

	PASSING						RUSHING				TOTAL
	CMP	ATT	YD	YPA	TD	INT	ATT	YD	YPA	TD	YD
TOTALS	339	528	4,021	7.62	27	12	511	2,257	4.42	17	6,278
NFL RANK	4	10	5	7	10	4	14	8	5	12	4

TEAM DEFENSE

	PASSING						RUSHING				TOTAL
	CMP	ATT	YD	YPA	TD	INT	ATT	YD	YPA	TD	YD
TOTALS	322	526	3,701	7.04	23	24	449	1,936	4.31	10	5,637
NFL RANK	27	22	19	11	18	10	6	10	21	4	13

Safety Ronnie Lott.
Michael Zagaris/Getty Images

Running back Wendell Tyler.
Ronald C. Modra/Getty Images

1984

RECORD 15-1

NFC WEST	W	L	T	W%	PF	PA
San Francisco 49ers	15	1	0	.938	475	227
Los Angeles Rams	10	6	0	.625	346	316
New Orleans Saints	7	9	0	.438	298	361
Atlanta Falcons	4	12	0	.250	281	382

SCHEDULE

Week 1	SFO	30	at DET	27
Week 2	WAS	31	at SFO	37
Week 3	NOR	20	at SFO	30
Week 4	SFO	21	at PHI	9
Week 5	ATL	5	at SFO	14
Week 6	SFO	31	at NYG	10
Week 7	PIT	20	at SFO	17
Week 8	SFO	34	at HOO	21
Week 9	SFO	33	at LAM	0
Week 10	CIN	17	at SFO	23
Week 11	SFO	41	at CLE	7
Week 12	TAM	17	at SFO	24
Week 13	SFO	35	at NOR	3
Week 14	SFO	35	at ATL	17
Week 15	MIN	7	at SFO	51
Week 16	LAM	16	at SFO	19
NFC Div. Playoff	NYG	10	at SFO	21
NFC Championship	CHI	0	at SFO	23
Super Bowl XIX	MIA	16	at SFO	38

1984 DRAFT

RND	PICK#	PLAYER, COLLEGE
1	24	Todd Shell, Brigham Young
2	56	John Frank, Ohio State
3	73	Guy McIntyre, Georgia
5	121	Michael Carter, Southern Methodist
5	139	Jeff Fuller, Texas A&M
9	239	Lee Miller, Cal-State Fullerton
9	248	Derrick Harmon, Cornell
10	275	Dave Moritz, Iowa
11	307	Kirk Pendleton, Brigham Young

TEAM OFFENSE

	PASSING						RUSHING				TOTAL
	CMP	ATT	YD	YPA	TD	INT	ATT	YD	YPA	TD	YD
TOTALS	312	496	4,079	8.22	32	10	534	2,465	4.62	21	6,544
NFL RANK	7	15	4	2	2	1	6	3	2	2	4

TEAM DEFENSE

	PASSING						RUSHING				TOTAL
	CMP	ATT	YD	YPA	TD	INT	ATT	YD	YPA	TD	YD
TOTALS	298	546	3,744	6.86	14	25	432	1,795	4.16	10	5,539
NFL RANK	15	22	19	9	2	7	3	7	21	6	9

SUPER BOWL XIX

JANUARY 20, 1985
STANFORD STADIUM · STANFORD, CALIFORNIA

	1	2	3	4	T
Miami Dolphins	10	6	0	0	16
San Francisco 49ers	7	21	10	0	38

In the stadium where Bill Walsh's head coaching career first began, the San Francisco 49ers pummeled the Miami Dolphins in one of the most lopsided Super Bowls ever played. Pitting one of the greatest quarterback matchups since the advent of passing-oriented offenses, Joe Montana proved mightier than the Dolphins' Dan Marino, spoiling the latter quarterback's only Super Bowl appearance. Montana garnered his second Super Bowl MVP trophy as the 49ers capped an astounding 18-1 season with an impressive offensive onslaught. Though the game ended in heavy favor of the 49ers, the opening minutes were as exciting as any memorable Super Bowl. The Dolphins struck first, taking their opening possession deep into 49er territory before settling for a field goal. San Francisco responded by scoring on a 33-yard touch down pass from Montana to Carl Monroe to finish a 78-yard drive. Marino countered by leading Miami to a touchdown using a no-huddle offense. By the end of the first quarter, the score was 10-7 in the Dolphins' favor, and the game looked as if it would be the shootout fans had expected. However, the San

Bill Walsh leads his team onto the field during Super Bowl XIX. *Ronald C. Modra/Getty Images*

Francisco offense took control while the 49er defense, headed by Pro Bowlers Ronnie Lott and Dwight Hicks, began to suffocate the Miami offense. The Dolphins could gain no momentum by ground—earning just 25 yards rushing on nine carries in the game. That forced Miami into a one-dimensional attack. San Francisco's defense anticipated the pass and put intense pressure on Marino, sacking the future Hall of Famer four times and intercepting him twice. On offense, Montana tallied four touchdowns—three in the air, one on the ground—331 yards passing, and a Super Bowl quarterback record 59 rushing yards. Walsh's West Coast system shattered the Super Bowl record for most yards in a game, totaling 537 yards and eclipsing the previous mark of 429 yards set by the Oakland Raiders. For the second time in less than five years the San Francisco 49ers were world champions, thus cementing the birth of a new dynasty.

OPPOSITE TOP: **Wendell Tyler carries the ball during Super Bowl XIX.** *Tony Duffy/Getty Images*

OPPOSITE BOTTOM: **Bill Walsh is carried off the field following Super Bowl XIX.** *George Rose/Getty Images*

Running back Roger Craig.
Jim Turner/NFL Images/Getty Images

1 9 8 5

RECORD 10-6

NFC WEST	W	L	T	W%	PF	PA
Los Angeles Rams	11	5	0	.688	340	277
San Francisco 49ers	**10**	**6**	**0**	**.625**	**411**	**263**
New Orleans Saints	5	11	0	.313	294	401
Atlanta Falcons	4	12	0	.250	282	452

SCHEDULE

Week 1	SFO	21	at MIN	28
Week 2	ATL	16	at SFO	35
Week 3	SFO	34	at LAD	10
Week 4	NOR	20	at SFO	17
Week 5	SFO	38	at ATL	17
Week 6	CHI	26	at SFO	10
Week 7	SFO	21	at DET	23
Week 8	SFO	28	at LAM	14
Week 9	PHI	13	at SFO	24
Week 10	SFO	16	at DEN	17
Week 11	KAN	3	at SFO	31
Week 12	SEA	6	at SFO	19
Week 13	SFO	35	at WAS	8
Week 14	LAM	27	at SFO	20
Week 15	SFO	31	at NOR	19
Week 16	DAL	16	at SFO	31
NFC Wild-Card	SFO	3	at NYG	17

1985 DRAFT

RND	PICK#	PLAYER, COLLEGE
1	16	Jerry Rice, Mississippi Valley State
3	75	Ricky Moore, Alabama
5	140	Bruce Collie, Texas-Arlington
6	168	Scott Barry, California-Davis
11	308	David Wood, Arizona
12	336	Donald Chumley, Georgia

TEAM OFFENSE

	PASSING						RUSHING				TOTAL
	CMP	ATT	YD	YPA	TD	INT	ATT	YD	YPA	TD	YD
TOTALS	331	550	3,987	7.25	28	14	477	2,232	4.68	20	6,219
NFL RANK	4	8	6	9	5	4	14	10	4	5	5

TEAM DEFENSE

	PASSING						RUSHING				TOTAL
	CMP	ATT	YD	YPA	TD	INT	ATT	YD	YPA	TD	YD
TOTALS	346	621	3,965	6.38	11	18	435	1,683	3.87	10	5,648
NFL RANK	27	28	23	5	1	20	5	7	8	5	15

Wide receiver Jerry Rice.
George Rose/Getty Images

1986

RECORD 10-5-1

NFC WEST	L	T	T	W%	PF	PA
Los Angeles Rams	10	6	0	.625	309	267
San Francisco 49ers	**10**	**5**	**1**	**.625**	**374**	**247**
Atlanta Falcons	7	8	1	.438	280	280
New Orleans Saints	7	9	0	.438	288	287

SCHEDULE

Week 1	SFO	31	at TAM	7
Week 2	SFO	13	at LAM	16
Week 3	NOR	17	at SFO	26
Week 4	SFO	31	at MIA	16
Week 5	IND	14	at SFO	35
Week 6	MIN	27	at SFO	24
Week 7	SFO	10	at ATL	10
Week 8	SFO	31	at GNB	17
Week 9	SFO	10	at NOR	23
Week 10	SLC	17	at SFO	43
Week 11	SFO	6	at WAS	14
Week 12	ATL	0	at SFO	20
Week 13	NYG	21	at SFO	17
Week 14	NYJ	10	at SFO	24
Week 15	SFO	29	at NWE	24
Week 16	LAM	14	at SFO	24
NFC Div. Playoff	SFO	3	at NYG	49

1986 DRAFT

RND	PICK#	PLAYER, COLLEGE
2	39	Larry Roberts, Alabama
3	56	Tom Rathman, Nebraska
3	64	Tim McKyer, Texas-Arlington
3	76	John Taylor, Delaware State
4	96	Charles Haley, James Madison
4	101	Steve Wallace, Auburn
4	102	Kevin Fagan, Miami (FL)
5	131	Patrick Miller, Florida
6	162	Don Griffin, Middle Tenn. State
8	203	Jim Popp, Vanderbilt
9	240	Tony Cherry, Oregon
10	267	Elliston Stinson, Rice
10	270	Harold Hallman, Auburn

TEAM OFFENSE

	PASSING						RUSHING				TOTAL
	CMP	ATT	YD	YPA	TD	INT	ATT	YD	YPA	TD	YD
TOTALS	353	582	4,299	7.39	21	20	510	1,986	3.89	16	6,285
NFL RANK	2	4	3	12	13	12	8	10	15	10	3

TEAM DEFENSE

	PASSING						RUSHING				TOTAL
	CMP	ATT	YD	YPA	TD	INT	ATT	YD	YPA	TD	YD
TOTALS	324	604	3,773	6.25	18	39	406	1,555	3.83	8	5,328
NFL RANK	24	28	18	2	8	1	2	3	14	2	11

Defensive tackle Michael Carter.
Michael Zagaris/Getty Images

1987

RECORD 13-2

NFC WEST	W	L	T	W%	PF	PA
San Francisco 49ers	13	2	0	.867	459	253
New Orleans Saints	12	3	0	.800	422	283
Los Angeles Rams	6	9	0	.400	317	361
Atlanta Falcons	3	12	0	.200	205	436

SCHEDULE

Week 1	SFO	17	at PIT	30
Week 2	SFO	27	at CIN	26
Week 4	SFO	41	at NYG	21
Week 5	SFO	25	at ATL	17
Week 6	SLC	28	at SFO	34
Week 7	SFO	24	at NOR	22
Week 8	SFO	31	at LAM	10
Week 9	HOO	20	at SFO	27
Week 10	NOR	26	at SFO	24
Week 11	SFO	24	at TAM	10
Week 12	CLE	24	at SFO	38
Week 13	SFO	23	at GNB	12
Week 14	CHI	0	at SFO	41
Week 15	ATL	7	at SFO	35
Week 16	LAM	0	at SFO	48
NFC Div. Playoff	MIN	36	at SFO	24

1987 DRAFT

RND	PICK#	PLAYER, COLLEGE
1	22	Harris Barton, North Carolina
1	25	Terrence Flagler, Clemson
2	37	Jeff Bregel, USC
5	134	Paul Jokisch, Michigan
6	162	Bob White, Penn State
7	189	Steve DeLine, Colorado State
8	217	David Grayson, Fresno State
9	245	Jonathan Shelley, Mississippi
10	275	John Paye, Stanford
11	301	Calvin Nicholas, Grambling

TEAM OFFENSE

	PASSING						RUSHING				TOTAL
	CMP	ATT	YD	YPA	TD	INT	ATT	YD	YPA	TD	YD
TOTALS	322	501	3,955	7.89	44	14	524	2,237	4.27	11	6,192
NFL RANK	2	10	2	1	1	3	3	1	4	20	1

TEAM DEFENSE

	PASSING						RUSHING				TOTAL
	CMP	ATT	YD	YPA	TD	INT	ATT	YD	YPA	TD	YD
TOTALS	224	467	2,771	5.93	13	25	429	1,611	3.76	8	4,382
NFL RANK	1	10	1	1	1	5	6	5	10	5	1

Quarterback Joe Montana.
Ron Vesely/Getty Images

1 9 8 8

RECORD 10-6

NFC WEST	W	L	T	W%	PF	PA
Los Angeles Rams	10	6	0	.625	407	293
New Orleans Saints	10	6	0	.625	312	283
San Francisco 49ers	**10**	**6**	**0**	**.625**	**369**	**294**
Atlanta Falcons	5	11	0	.313	244	315

SCHEDULE

Week 1	SFO	34	at NOR	33
Week 2	SFO	20	at NYG	17
Week 3	ATL	34	at SFO	17
Week 4	SFO	38	at SEA	7
Week 5	DET	13	at SFO	20
Week 6	DEN	16	at SFO	13
Week 7	SFO	24	at LAM	21
Week 8	SFO	9	at CHI	10
Week 9	MIN	21	at SFO	24
Week 10	SFO	23	at PHO	24
Week 11	LAD	9	at SFO	3
Week 12	WAS	21	at SFO	37
Week 13	SFO	48	at SDG	10
Week 14	SFO	13	at ATL	3
Week 15	NOR	17	at SFO	30
Week 16	LAM	38	at SFO	16
NFC Div. Playoff	MIN	9	at SFO	34
NFC Championship	SFO	28	at CHI	3
Super Bowl XXIII	CIN	16	at SFO	20

1988 DRAFT

RND	PICK#	PLAYER, COLLEGE
2	33	Daniel Stubbs, Miami (FL)
2	39	Pierce Holt, Angelo State
3	80	Bill Romanowski, Boston College
4	102	Barry Helton, Colorado
7	191	Kevin Bryant, Delaware State
8	219	Larry Clarkson, Montana
9	247	Brian Bonner, Minnesota
10	275	Tim Foley, Georgia Southern
11	303	Chet Brooks, Texas A&M
12	331	Georga Mira Jr., Miami (FL)

TEAM OFFENSE

	PASSING						RUSHING				TOTAL
	CMP	ATT	YD	YPA	TD	INT	ATT	YD	YPA	TD	YD
TOTALS	293	502	3,675	7.32	21	14	527	2,523	4.79	18	6,198
NFL RANK	12	15	11	9	11	3	7	2	2	7	3

TEAM DEFENSE

	PASSING						RUSHING				TOTAL
	CMP	ATT	YD	YPA	TD	INT	ATT	YD	YPA	TD	YD
TOTALS	292	530	3,284	6.20	25	22	441	1,588	3.60	8	4,872
NFL RANK	20	22	8	2	25	7	5	3	4	4	3

SUPER BOWL XXIII

JANUARY 22, 1989
JOE ROBBIE STADIUM · MIAMI, FLORIDA

	1	2	3	4	T
Cincinnati Bengals	0	3	10	3	16
San Francisco 49ers	3	0	3	14	20

It had been four years since the San Francisco 49ers' last Super Bowl appearance, though not for lack of effort. Bill Walsh's squad had made the playoffs all three seasons since winning Super Bowl XIX following the 1984 season, but had failed to win a postseason game, losing to the Giants in 1985 and '86, and the Vikings in 1987. Doubters abounded following a 10-6 regular season, despite the emergence of Jerry Rice as an elite wide receiver and the dominance of veteran Roger Craig, who in his sixth NFL season posted his highest rushing yardage total with 1,502 yards. But this time around, the 49ers were up to the task of silencing their critics. The team took care of Minnesota with ease in their playoff opener, 34-9, then wiped out Chicago, 28-3. That set up a rematch of Super Bowl XVI, San Francisco versus Cincinnati. Before the Bengals even stepped on the field of play, they were dealt a crushing blow when running back Stanley Wilson was busted for drugs in his hotel room on the eve of the big game. But even without Wilson, the Bengals posed a formidable offensive threat, led by a resilient running attack featuring Ickey Woods and James Brooks plus quarterback Boomer Esiason, that season's NFL MVP. The game was a back-and-forth battle that headed into halftime with the score tied 3-3. Cincinnati found itself with the ball late in the fourth quarter and the scored tied 13-13. Bengals kicker Jim Breech sailed a 40-yard field goal through the uprights to give his team a 16-13 advantage with only 3:20 remaining in the game. It was time for Montana to earn his third Super Bowl ring and solidify his stature as one of the greatest fourth-quarter QBs of all time. In a possession simply remembered as "The Drive," Montana calmly advanced San Francisco 92 yards on 11 plays for the winning score, utilizing his receivers and running backs to perfection. The Drive ended with a 10-yard touchdown pass to John Taylor with just over half a minute remaining. The Bengals, who were limited to just 229 total yards in the game, were unable to move the ball on their final possession, sealing the deal for Walsh to go out on top. The veteran coach announced his retirement after the game, thus commencing a game-changing coaching career. Jerry Rice, who took home the first of his Super Bowl rings, was named Super Bowl MVP for his record-setting 215-yard receiving performance.

OPPOSITE TOP: Joe Montana in action during Super Bowl XXIII. *Mike Powell/Allsport/Getty Images*

OPPOSITE BOTTOM: Greg Cox (left) and Bill Romanowski celebrate the 49ers victory in Super Bowl XXIII. *Andy Hayt/Getty Images*

ROGER CRAIG ON BILL WALSH

In many ways, Coach Walsh still is the 49ers.

Everything the organization accomplished in the 1980s can be traced back to him. He had the vision and the strength to put his plan into place. Owner Eddie DeBartolo stepped aside and let Coach Walsh do what he did best—acquire the players to best fit his "West Coast Offense." I just wish Coach Walsh had remained as the coach of the 49ers for a few more years. . . .

I had a special bond with Coach Walsh. He is the only coach I ever had who knew exactly how to utilize my skills. He knew more about my attributes as a player than I did.

I had nothing bad to say about Coach Walsh when I was playing for him, and I have nothing bad to say about him now. He is the greatest tactician in the history of the National Football League.

What more needs to be said about his ability on the sideline? He inherited a team that went 2-14 in 1978. Three seasons later, he became the first head coach to wear headsets on the sideline—a true indicator of his involvement in the down-to-down strategy of his team. Coach Walsh provided the NFL and the 49ers with a fresh approach. To him, the game of football was a chess match. When we went onto the field, we knew we would always be better prepared than our opponent, and that was half the battle right there.

From 1981 to his retirement after the 1988 season, he won Super Bowls in three of the six non-strike seasons. And with his players and system firmly entrenched, we won another Super Bowl the year after his retirement with George Seifert as coach.

Running back Roger Craig. *Otto Greule Jr./Allsport/Getty Images*

He would certainly prove that he was smart enough to run an entire franchise. He was the president, general manager and coach. Owner Eddie DeBartolo demanded everybody perform to the highest possible level, from the coaches on down to the equipment manager. But then he stepped aside and let Coach Walsh run the show. That's how our dynasty was built. Coach Walsh ran the organization from the marketing down to giving the players contracts.

Coach Walsh commanded respect. I feared him, but I also had—and still have—immeasurable respect for him. He is a special man. ✦

From *Roger Craig's Tales from the San Francisco 49ers Sideline*
By Roger Craig
with Matt Maiocco

Joe Montana high-fives Jerry Rice on the sideline.
Michael Zagaris/Getty Images

PRO BOWLERS UNDER WALSH

NAME	POSITION	YEARS
Michael Carter	DT	'85, '87, '88
Dwight Clark	WR	'81, '82
Roger Craig	FB/RB	'85, '87, '88
Randy Cross	DE	'81, '82, '84
Fred Dean	G	'81, '83
Keith Fahnhorst	T	'84
Charles Haley	LB/DE	'88
Dwight Hicks	S	'81, '82, '83, '84
Ronnie Lott	CB	'81, '82, '83, '84, '86, '87, '88
Joe Montana	QB	'81, '83, '84, '85, '87, '88
Fred Quillan	C	'84, '85
Jerry Rice	WR	'86, '87, '88
Keena Turner	LB	'84
Wendell Tyler	RB	'84
Carlton Williamson	S	'84, '85
Eric Wright	CB	'84, '85

BILL WALSH, FROM HIS PRO FOOTBALL HALL OF FAME INDUCTION SPEECH

I was the fifth coach in just a matter of years trying to find the right formula, but we found it. In three years we found it. The first year, I was sure we would win our share. We won two and lost 14 and believe me when you go through that, you soul search. The next year, there were posters all over the city because we won our first three games. We won our first game on the road in 27 tries in San Francisco. One out of 27, I was proud of it, roaring back only to lose the next eight games in a row. . . .

I looked out the window for five hours in the middle of the night because I broke down emotionally. I had conceded that I couldn't get the job done. Fourteen losses the first year, eight straight the next year. When you lose eight straight you don't think you'll ever win again. Eight straight loses; I had conceded it. When I got off the plane I was thinking I'll finish the year out, I'll go to Ed Jr. and talk to him about maybe being some sort of management for him 'cause I brought it this far and I can't get it all the way.

Well, we won the next game. And we won the next game. And we won the next game. And the next year we were world champions. So in three years we turned the whole thing around. . . .

At one point San Francisco was in the absolute doldrums, morale wise. There had just been an assassination of the mayor and . . . the city was ridiculed by many people. Well after three years we had a victory parade through Market Street. We turned the corner and there were 300,000 people. And my point is there were older people and younger people. There were black people, white people. There were Asian people. There were rich people and rather poor people. There were people of every gender, every interest, all of the sudden, the city came together. The city became San Francisco again. The city became a world champion for the first time and all of those kinds of things were forgotten and minimized because we had with the San Francisco 49ers turned an entire state around and a huge and great city around because of professional football. ✦

GEORGE SEIFERT
Defensive backs coach under Walsh in 1980 before becoming defensive coordinator in 1983. In 1989, succeeded Walsh as head coach and won two Super Bowls with 49ers.

BRUCE COSLET
Played under Walsh on the Cincinnati Bengals, where Walsh was an assistant. Became an assistant for Walsh from 1980-85.

DENNIS GREEN
Assistant for Walsh at Stanford. In 1985 became running backs coach for Walsh in San Francisco. Preceded Walsh's second stint at Stanford, coaching the Cardinals from 1989-91.

JEFF FISHER

GARY KUBIAK

MIKE TICE

SCOTT LINEHAN

JON GRUDEN

MIKE SHANAHAN

BRIAN BILLICK

TONY DUNGY

BILL CALLAHAN

JACK DEL RIO

MARVIN LEWIS

MIKE NOLAN

BILL WALSH
COACHING TREE

Bill Walsh molded his West Coast Offense on research from a variety of sources. He began by studying longtime Chargers coach Sid Gillman's playbook. Al Davis gave Walsh his first NFL coaching job with the Raiders, then taught him the intricacies of Gillman's offense. Later, Walsh would add to those models as an assistant under the Bengals' Paul Brown. In time, Walsh's offense would prove revolutionary, and a host of new coaches would study him.

RAY RHODES
Played for Walsh for final two seasons of his career in 1979 and 1980. Became assistant secondary coach for Walsh immediately after retiring and then served as defensive backs coach for 49ers until 1991.

SEAN PAYTON

SAM WYCHE
Served as assistant coach in charge of directing the passing game for Walsh's 49ers from 1979-82.

MIKE MULARKEY

MIKE HOLMGREN
Quarterbacks coach for Walsh at San Francisco from 1982-88. Credited with developing Joe Montana and Steve Young.

DICK JURON

MIKE SHERMAN

MARTY MORNHINWEG

ANDY REID

BRAD CHILDRESS

ROD MARINELLI

MIKE TOMLIN

LOVIE SMITH

HERM EDWARDS

ON FOOTBALL: "THE GENIUS" TRULY WAS ONE

————BY DAVE GOLDBERG, AP FOOTBALL WRITER————

Bill Walsh might have been the first football coach given the label "genius." He deserved it—and not just with Xs and Os.

Yes, Walsh designed the "West Coast offense"—used by dozens of NFL teams, imitated by dozens of coaches the last 25 years and credited for San Francisco's five Super Bowl victories. But the man who died at age 75 was as well-rounded a football man as there has ever been—on and off the field.

Not only did he take an offense taught to him by Sid Gilman when he was an assistant in Cincinnati, but he innovated within that offense.

"The Drive," which culminated with the Joe Montana-to-Dwight Clark TD pass that put the 49ers in their first Super Bowl in January 1982 was a masterpiece of playcalling that featured more runs than passes as the Dallas team expected Montana to throw, throw, throw.

"He had everything broken down into real refined detail, the ways guys did things," said Howard Mudd, the Colts' offensive line coach, who was a fledgling coach when Walsh was an assistant in San Diego developing Hall of Fame quarterback Dan Fouts. "And yet, he didn't make them real mechanical men. He'd take quarterbacks who could run and let them run. He'd take quarterbacks that couldn't run and let them sit in the pocket."

But for Walsh, there was always so much more than football.

He was one of the first to realize the importance of getting black players into coaching.

"He was just a very socially conscious guy," said Tony Dungy, the first black coach to win a Super Bowl. Dungy, who played one year for Walsh, was traded to the New York Giants for Ray Rhodes, whom Walsh later added to his coaching staff and eventually became one of the NFL's first black coaches.

Another strength, perhaps Walsh's greatest, was judging talent.

Even his failures succeeded.

By several accounts, he had to be convinced by chief scout Tony Razzano to take Montana with a third-round pick in his first draft in 1979.

But in 1985, he jumped up from 28th, last in the first round, to 16 to take a receiver named Jerry Rice, whose stock had fallen because he had run the 40-yard dash in a mediocre 4.6 seconds in workouts.

A year later, he had what many people consider the best draft ever—John Taylor, Tom Rathman, Tim McKyer, Larry Roberts, Steve Wallace, Kevin Fagan, Don Griffin and Charles Haley. All major contributors, their teams won two Super Bowls. Haley, later traded to Dallas, won three more titles with the Cowboys.

Walsh had an equally good eye for coaching talent.

He knew where to look—such as Brigham Young, which during Walsh's early years with the 49ers had perhaps the most sophisticated passing game in college football.

In 1979, he hired former BYU tight end Brian Billick, who impressed him in an interview. Walsh didn't have a slot on his coaching staff so he put Billick on the public relations payroll—though reporters who covered the team in those days remember Billick as a coaching intern rather than a PR man.

But Walsh's most important BYU hire (unless you count the trade in which he stole Steve Young from Tampa) was Mike Holmgren, a former San Francisco high school coach whom Walsh hired in 1986. Holmgren became the 49ers offensive coordinator, replaced by Mike Shanahan. As head coach in Green Bay and Seattle, Holmgren spun off Jon Gruden, Steve Mariucci, Rhodes and Andy Reid, another BYU grad.

Dungy's not part of that coaching tree but playing for Walsh in 1979 certainly left a mark.

Michael Zagaris/Getty Images

"I LEARNED AN AWFUL LOT IN ONE YEAR [PLAYING FOR WALSH IN 1979]."

— TONY DUNGY

"He never focused on what guys couldn't do, and if you weren't good at one thing, it didn't really matter because he was not afraid to substitute and use all 22 or 23 players on offense," Dungy said Monday. "He was very much under control and professorial, and that's something I really appreciated. I learned an awful lot in one year."

That's the ultimate legacy.

Almost every coach and player who had contact with Walsh considers him a teacher.

So does the commissioner.

"If you gave him a blackboard and a piece of chalk, he would become a whirlwind of wisdom," Roger Goodell said. "He taught all of us not only about football but also about life and how it takes teamwork for any of us to succeed as individuals." ✦

Michael Zagaris/Getty Images

ROGER CRAIG ON THE END OF THE BILL WALSH ERA IN SAN FRANCISCO

Our locker room was quite joyous after [our victory in Super Bowl XXIII]. Everybody had to think that the 49ers were going to finally lose a Super Bowl, and we managed to pull it out with a pressure-packed final drive.

While I was celebrating with some teammates, broadcaster Brent Musburger was interviewing Coach Walsh on the podium. He asked Coach Walsh if this were, indeed, his final game as coach of the 49ers. Coach Walsh began to cry. It wasn't until later that evening I found out that Coach Walsh had retired as coach of the 49ers. I didn't know he was going to do that. He surprised all of us.

Coach Walsh understood me as a player better than any coach I'd ever had. He knew my strengths and my weaknesses, and he knew how to utilize my skills to best serve the team. When he retired, a part of me died. I wasn't the same running back after he stepped down as coach.

Of course, looking back on it, Coach Walsh stepped away too soon. He was still a great coach and he had a lot more years left in him. We won the Super Bowl the following year under George Seifert, but it wasn't George's team. Only after Joe Montana left and Steve Young came in as the full-time starter did it truly become George's team. . . . ✦

From *Roger Craig's Tales from the San Francisco 49ers Sideline* By Roger Craig with Matt Maiocco

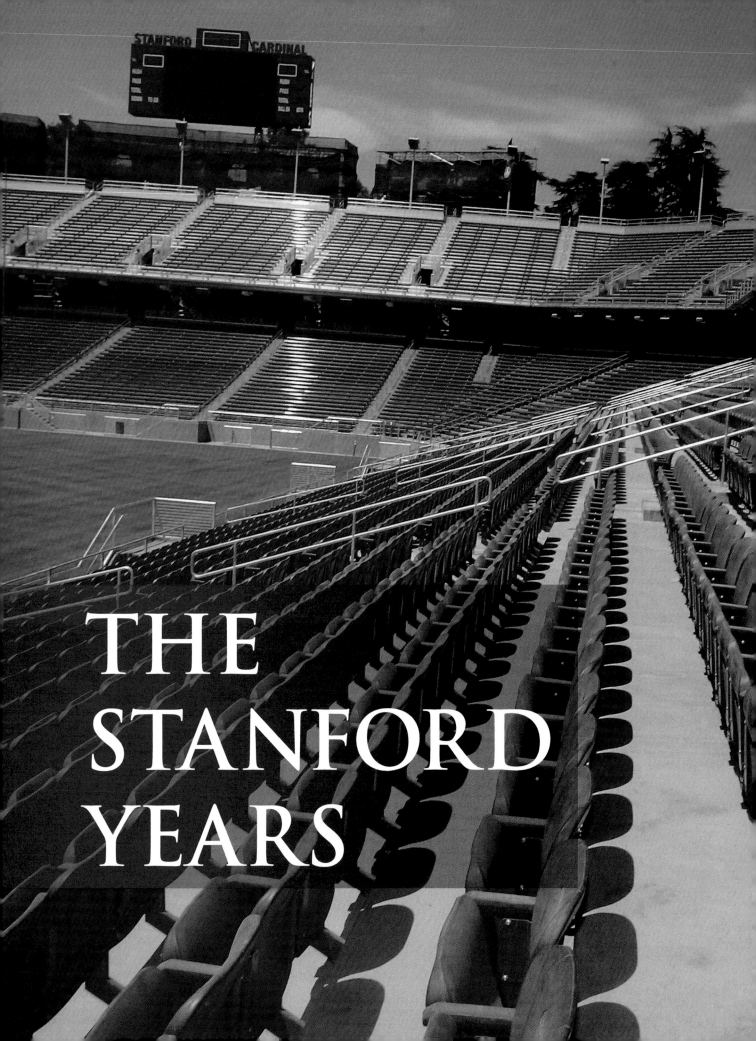

THE STANFORD YEARS

David Gonzales/Icon SMI

BILL WALSH'S
CARDINAL CONNECTION

B ill Walsh had three tours of duty at Stanford. His first came in 1963, when then-coach John Ralston hired him as an assistant coach. In 1966, he left college football and began his career in the NFL as an assistant coach with the Oakland Raiders. But the place that had given him part of his football foundation called him back in 1977, when athletic director Joe Ruetz hired Walsh as the Cardinal's new head football coach. It was the first head-coaching position Walsh had ever held, and he was more than ready for the challenge.

In his first year in charge, Walsh guided Stanford to its finest season since 1971 and was named Pac-8 Coach of the Year. His accomplishments that year included leading the Cardinal to a 9-3 overall record, a No. 15 national ranking, and a 24-14 win over LSU in the Sun Bowl, held on December 31 in El Paso, Texas. The bowl game pitted the explosive Cardinal passing attack, led by All-America quarterback Guy Benjamin, freshman sensation Darrin Nelson at running back, and All-Pac 8 receiver James Lofton, against the potent LSU running attack, led by their All-America running back, Charles Alexander.

Stanford tied the game at 7-7 early in the second quarter on a 49-yard pass play from Benjamin to Lofton, but a seven-yard run by Alexander with less that a minute to play in the first half put LSU on top 14-10 at halftime.

The second half, however, belonged to Walsh and his Cardinal team. Stanford linebacker Gordy Ceresino and the rest of the defense shut out the powerful LSU offense, and Walsh's offense put up two touchdowns in the second half. Ceresino finished the game with 22 tackles and was named the Defensive MVP. Benjamin, the game's Offensive MVP, finished 23-for-36 for 269 yards passing, three touchdowns, and no interceptions. The game was monumental for two other reasons: Benjamin set a Sun Bowl record for passing; and LSU's Alexander, with 197 yards on the ground, set the bowl record for rushing.

Walsh's next season as head coach ended in a second consecutive bowl appearance—this time versus Georgia in the Bluebonnet Bowl. The game is widely known as of the greatest comebacks in Stanford football history. The Bulldogs were leading 22-0 early in the third quarter when Walsh began calling a Cardinal comeback.

Over a six-and-a-half-minute span late in the third quarter and early in the fourth, Stanford scored 25 unanswered points. With 6:03 left in the third period, Stanford quarterback Steve Dils hit wide receiver Ken Margerum on a 32-yard touchdown pass play. Dils next hit running back Darrin Nelson on a 20-yard touchdown pass play with 3:57 remaining in the quarter, then connected with Margerum again from 14 yards out with 1:33 left in the quarter. A two-point conversion tied the score at 22-22. Placekicker Ken Naber's 24-yard field goal completed the comeback and put the Cardinal ahead to stay, thanks in part to Defensive MVP Gordy Ceresino, who accounted for 20 tackles.

Fourteen years passed between the Bluebonnet Bowl victory and Walsh's next stint as Stanford's head football coach. Of course, he put those years to good use, becoming the architect of the San Francisco 49ers for 10 seasons, where he won three Super Bowl championships and was dubbed "The Genius" for his innovations that changed the game of football. Along the way, he was named the NFL's Coach of the Decade for the 1980s, and in 1993, Walsh was elected to the Professional Football Hall of Fame, becoming only the 14th coach in history to be elected to the Hall.

Three years after leaving pro football following the 1988 season, Walsh returned to Stanford in 1992 after deciding to come out of retirement and return as the head football coach once again. The official announcement, which was made on January 16, 1992, came after several closed-door meetings between Stanford Athletic Director Ted Leland, prominent Stanford alums, and Walsh himself. Walsh took the position after some soul-searching: "I knew that if I was ever to resume my coaching career, it would be at Stanford," he once said.

The press conference to announce Walsh's return seemed more like a coronation ceremony than a news gathering. Over 600 people packed into Burnham

Bill Walsh recruited John Elway to Stanford, but left for the NFL prior to Elway's freshman season in 1979. *AP Images*

Pavilion to get a glimpse of Walsh. The Stanford Band was there to provide the soundtrack, and the Dollies—the band's dancing version of cheerleaders—performed various routines. Even some of Stanford's professors had wandered over to Burnham to be part of the action. Television cameras lined the Pavilion; ESPN carried the event live to a national audience.

"I missed coaching," Walsh said at the news conference. "I missed working with young men, being a part of something from the inside. But it really hadn't hit me until the Stanford opportunity happened."

Walsh's touch worked its magic once again in '92. The Cardinal finished 10-3, beat Penn State in the Blockbuster Bowl, and ended the season ranked ninth in the nation, Stanford's first top-10 ranking since 1970. One game in particular stood out from that year for Walsh— a matchup with Notre Dame.

Stanford, 3-1 and ranked 18th nationally, went into South Bend, Indiana, on October 3 to face a team that was 4-0 and ranked sixth in the country. Walsh had been to South Bend for a football game on many occasions since retiring as head coach of the San Francisco 49ers, having worked as a commentator for NBC's coverage of Notre Dame home games. But on that day, Walsh led his team to an improbable 33-16

Bill Walsh is lifted into the air by his players after Stanford's win in the 1978 Bluebonnet Bowl.
AP Images

win—Stanford's second consecutive upset win in South Bend.

The game's opening drive gave little indication of Stanford's eventual victory. Notre Dame sacked Stanford quarterback Steve Stenstrom on the first play, then drove 55 yards on its opening possession and quickly led 9-0. A second-quarter touchdown put the Irish on top 16-0. But just when things looked their worst, Walsh turned his team around. The Cardinal followed the Notre Dame touchdown with 33 unanswered points of their own, leaving no doubt as to who was the better team that day.

"Our win over Notre Dame in 1992 ranks with any Super Bowl victory that I have ever experienced," Walsh said in his foreword to *Stanford: Home of Champions*.

Walsh stayed on as Stanford head coach until 1994, and although the team's record never matched their earlier success, the Cardinal did beat nationally ranked Colorado in 1993 and Washington in 1994, two games that Walsh has said rank as high on his list as any regular-season NFL game.

After serving as the 49ers general manager from 1999-2001, Walsh eventually returned to Stanford yet again, this time joining the faculty of the Graduate School of Business and helping to teach a course in sports business management. He was also critical to the formation of

Bill Walsh hoists the Bluebonnet Bowl trophy in 1978.

AP Images

the NFL-Stanford Executive Education Program in the Graduate School.

Walsh's role on the football field transformed as well when, in 2004, he was appointed as special assistant to Stanford's athletic director. After Ted Leland stepped down from the position in 2005, Walsh took over as the interim athletic director.

Of his time at Stanford, Walsh wrote in *Stanford: Home of Champions,* "I have experienced my ultimate gratification and satisfaction in the camaraderie, mutual commitment, sacrifice, and personal relationships while a member of the Athletic Department at Stanford University." Just as his influence continues to permeate much of the NFL, Bill Walsh will forever remain an important and honored figure in the Stanford community. ✦

BILL WALSH
AT STANFORD

YEAR	W-L	PF	PA	CAPTAINS
1977	9-3	285	279	Guy Benjamin (QB); Gordy Ceresino (LB)
1978	8-4	326	221	Gordy Ceresino (LB); Steve Dils (QB)
1992	10-3	296	193	Appointed by game
1993	4-7	291	389	Appointed by game
1994	3-7-1	327	359	Appointed by game

1977 9-3 (Walsh named Pac-8 Coach of the Year)

DATE	OPPONENT	W/L	SCORE
Sept. 10	at Colorado	L	27-21
Sept. 17	at Tulane	W	21-17
Sep. 24	Illinois	W	37-24
Oct. 1	Oregon	W	20-10
Oct. 8	UCLA	W	32-28
Oct. 15	at Washington	L	45-21
Oct. 22	Washington State	W	31-29
Oct. 29	at Oregon State	W	26-7
Nov. 5	at USC	L	49-0
Nov. 12	San Jose State	W	31-26
Nov. 19	California	W	21-3
Dec. 31	LSU (Sun Bowl)	W	24-14

1978 8-4

DATE	OPPONENT	W/L	SCORE
Sept. 9	Oklahoma	L	35-29
Sept. 16	San Jose State	W	38-9
Sept. 23	at Illinois	W	35-10
Sept. 30	Tulane	W	17-14
Oct. 7	at UCLA	L	27-26
Oct. 14	Washington	L	34-31
Oct. 21	at Washington State	W	43-27
Oct. 28	Oregon State	W	24-6
Nov. 4	USC	L	13-7
Nov. 11	at Arizona State	W	21-14
Nov. 18	at California	W	30-10
Dec. 31	Georgia (Bluebonnet Bowl)	W	25-22

1992 10-3

DATE	OPPONENT	W/L	SCORE
Aug. 26	Texas A&M	L	10-7
Sept. 12	Oregon	W	21-7
Sept. 19	Northwestern	W	35-24
Sept. 26	San Jose State	W	37-13
Oct. 3	at Notre Dame	W	33-16
Oct. 10	at UCLA	W	19-7
Oct. 17	Arizona	L	21-6
Oct. 24	at Oregon State	W	27-21
Oct. 31	at Washington	L	41-7
Nov. 7	USC	W	23-9
Nov. 14	Washington State	W	40-3
Nov. 21	at California	W	41-21
Jan. 1	Penn State (Blockbuster Bowl)	W	24-3

1993 4-7

DATE	OPPONENT	W/L	SCORE
Sept. 4	at Washington	L	31-14
Sept. 11	San Jose State	W	31-28
Sept. 18	Colorado	W	41-37
Sept. 25	UCLA	L	28-25
Oct. 2	Notre Dame	L	48-20
Oct. 16	at Arizona	L	27-24
Oct. 23	Arizona State	L	38-30
Oct. 30	Oregon State	W	31-27
Nov. 6	at USC	L	45-20
Nov. 13	at Oregon	W	38-34
Nov. 20	California	L	46-17

1994 3-7-1

Date	Opponent	W/L	Score
Sept. 10	at Northwestern	T	41-41
Sept. 17	San Jose State	W	51-20
Sept. 24	Arizona	L	34-10
Oct. 1	at Notre Dame	L	34-15
Oct. 8	at Arizona State	L	36-35
Oct. 15	USC	L	27-20
Oct. 22	at Oregon State	W	35-29
Oct. 29	at UCLA	L	31-30
Nov. 5	Washington	W	46-28
Nov. 12	Oregon	L	55-21
Nov. 19	at California	L	24-23

HONORS UNDER WALSH
AT STANFORD

All-America Selections
1977
Guy Benjamin, QB
Gordon King, OT

1992
Ron George, OLB
Glyn Milburn, RB

All-Conference Selections
1977
Guy Benjamin, QB
Gordy Ceresino, LB
Gordon King, OT
James Lofton, WR
Darrin Nelson, RB

1978
Gordy Ceresino, LB
Ken Margerum, WR
Darrin Nelson, RB

1992
Ron George, OLB
John Lynch, FS
Glyn Milburn, RB

1994
Justin Armour, WR

Miscellaneous Honors

Pac-10 Player of the Year
1977
Guy Benjamin, QB
(shared with Warren Moon, QB, Wash.)

Rhodes Scholar
1992
Cory Booker, TE

Pop Warner Trophy
1977
Guy Benjamin, QB

1992
Glyn Milburn, RB

1994
Steve Stenstrum

College Football Hall of Fame
James Lofton, WR, 1974-77

David Gonzales/Icon SMI

Thanks Coach Walsh!
We will miss you!

AP Images

PLAYERS, FANS PAY TRIBUTE TO FORMER 49ERS COACH BILL WALSH

BY SUDHIN THANAWALA,
AP WRITER

A grateful city said goodbye to Bill Walsh on Friday by making sure his name will stay forever linked to the field at Candlestick Park.

Hundreds gathered there to celebrate Walsh, who died of leukemia on July 30 at 75. Friday's service included a gospel choir singing "Amazing Graze" and a video recounting Walsh's achievements.

San Francisco Mayor Gavin Newsom told the crowd Friday the field at Monster Park would be named after Bill Walsh although the name of the stadium won't change.

"He shared his action, he shared his passion, and he made our lives better," Newsom said.

Several of the players key to Walsh's three Super Bowl championships with San Francisco—Jerry Rice, Steve Young and Joe Montana—attended the event.

"He helped us climb the mountain to the championship," Young, said. "He made us all feel like champions."

Walsh revolutionized many aspects of the game, most notably by deploying a system of short, precise passes, during a decade as the team's coach. He won 10 of his 14 postseason games and ended with a record of 102-63-1.

His 1981 team won the city's first Super Bowl and produced one of the most memorable moments in NFL history when Dwight Clark leapt high into the air at Candlestick to snare a high pass from Montana for a touchdown with 51 seconds the NFC Championship game.

The 49ers went on to beat Cincinnati in the Super Bowl.

"He built the dynasty that all of us fans got to enjoy," said Dante Stevens, 43,

"I DON'T THINK HE KNOWS HOW MUCH WE LOVED HIM."

—JOE MONTANA

who wore a 49ers jersey and took a day off from work as a chef to attend the memorial.

Stevens said Walsh was gifted at spotting talented players.

"It's hard to say whether any other coach will top this guy," said Mike Lopez, 49, who drove from San Jose for the event.

Other speakers at Friday's memorial service recalled how Walsh and the 49ers uplifted the city during turbulent times.

Sen. Dianne Feinstein said San Francisco was reeling from the assassinations of Mayor George Moscone and Supervisor Harvey Milk, the emerging HIV epidemic, and the massacre of roughly 900 Californians in Jonestown.

She recalled watching Montana's famous pass to Dwight Clark to win the 1981 NFC Championship Game.

"What that meant for this city to win something, to do something right," Feinstein said.

Montana said before his death, Walsh asked him to tell the players how much he loved them.

"But I don't think he knows how much we loved him," Montana said. "On behalf of all the players, Coach: We love you and are going to miss you." ✦

OPPOSITE TOP: Thousands of 49ers fans gather at Walsh's public memorial on August 10, 2007. *Justin Sullivan/Getty Images*

OPPOSITE BOTTOM: Joe Montana speaks to the crowd at Walsh's public memorial. *Justin Sullivan/Getty Images*

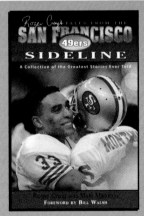
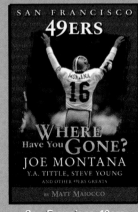
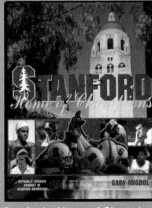